GUIDE TO WEREWOLVES

A Crabtree Branches Book

BY CARRIE GLEASON

Crabtree Publishing
crabtreebooks.com

Developed and produced by Plan B Book Packagers
www.planbbookpackagers.com
Art director: Rosie Gowsell Pattison

Crabtree editor: Ellen Rodger
Proofreader: Melissa Boyce
Production manager: Candice Campbell
Prepress technician: Katherine Kantor

Photographs:
p. 7 (low), p. 8-9, p. 16 (right): Rosie Gowsell Pattison.
All other images Shutterstock.com.

Crabtree Publishing

crabtreebooks.com 800-387-7650

In Canada: We acknowledge the financial support of the Government of Canada through the Canada Book Fund for our publishing activities.

Hardcover: 978-1-0396-6348-0
Paperback: 978-1-0396-6397-8
Ebook (pdf): 978-1-0396-6840-9
Epub: 978-1-0396-8580-2

Published in Canada
Crabtree Publishing
616 Welland Avenue
St. Catharines, Ontario
L2M 5V6

Published in the United States Crabtree Publishing
347 Fifth Avenue
Suite 1402-145
New York, NY 10016

Library and Archives Canada Cataloguing in Publication
Available at Library and Archives Canada

Library of Congress Cataloging-in-Publication Data
Available at the Library of Congress

Printed in the U.S.A./072025/CP20250721

CONTENTS

Cryptids and Kinfolk............. 4

Fear the Werewolf................. 6

Anatomy of a Werewolf.......... 8

The Way of the Werewolf 10

Werewolves Around the World.......................... 12

Transformation 14

Shapeshifters.......................16

How to Stop a Werewolf....... 18

The Legends Begin 20

Werewolves on Trial........... 22

Werewolves Make It Big 24

Humanoid Cryptids 26

Werewolves and Dogmen Sighted!............................ 28

Werewolves Explained......... 30

Learning More..................... 31

Glossary and Index 32

CRYPTIDS and KINFOLK

This chart shows some of the best-known cryptids and creatures from folklore. How many of them do you think are real?

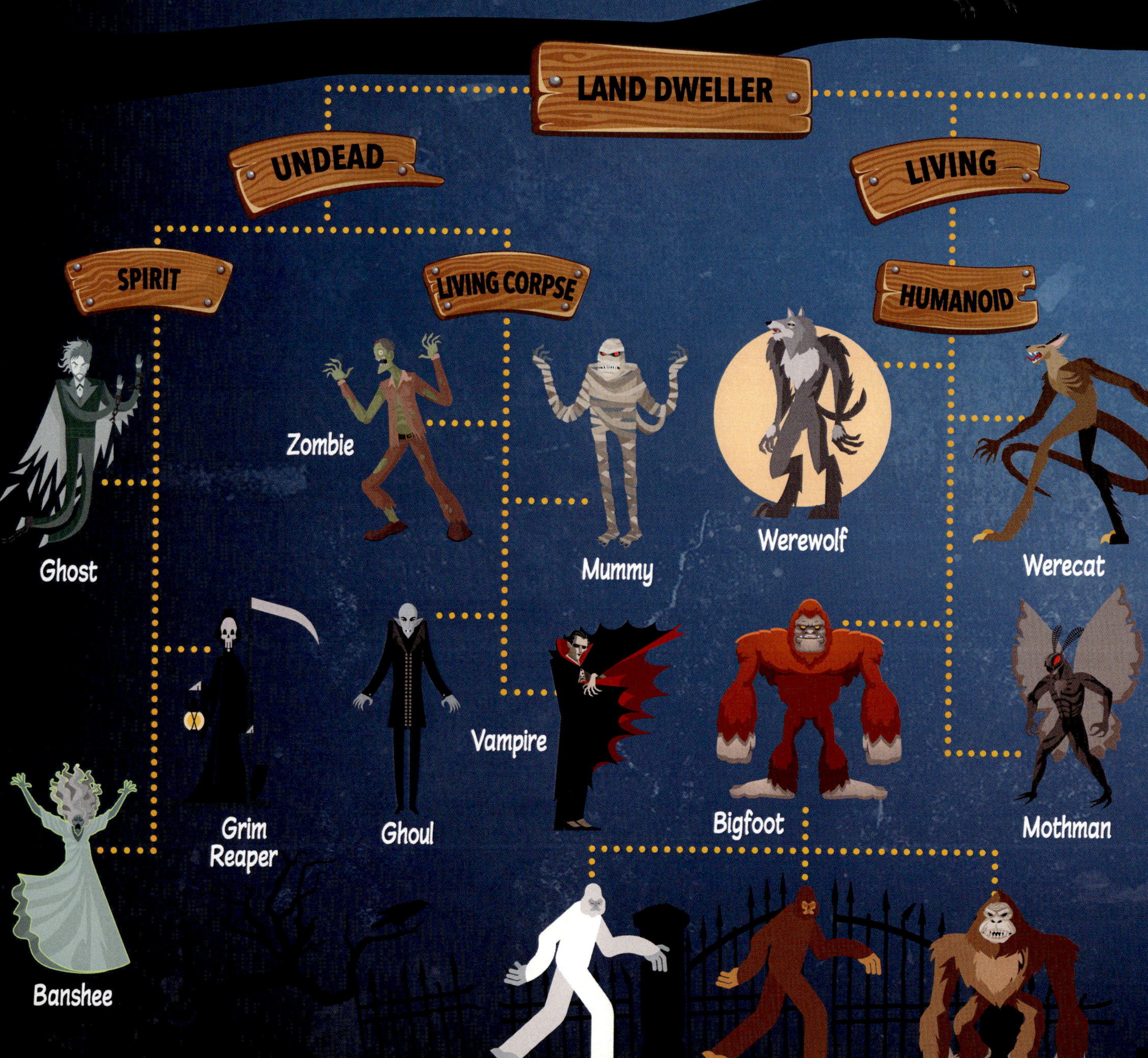

WHAT IS A WEREWOLF?

A werewolf is a cryptid—a creature from folklore whose existence is not yet proven to be true. Cryptozoologists are people who search for, and study these creatures. They gather stories from folklore and investigate reported sightings of cryptids. This book shows what is true, what is thought to be true, and what are outright lies and hoaxes about werewolves. Could werewolves be real? This Cryptid Guide will help you decide!

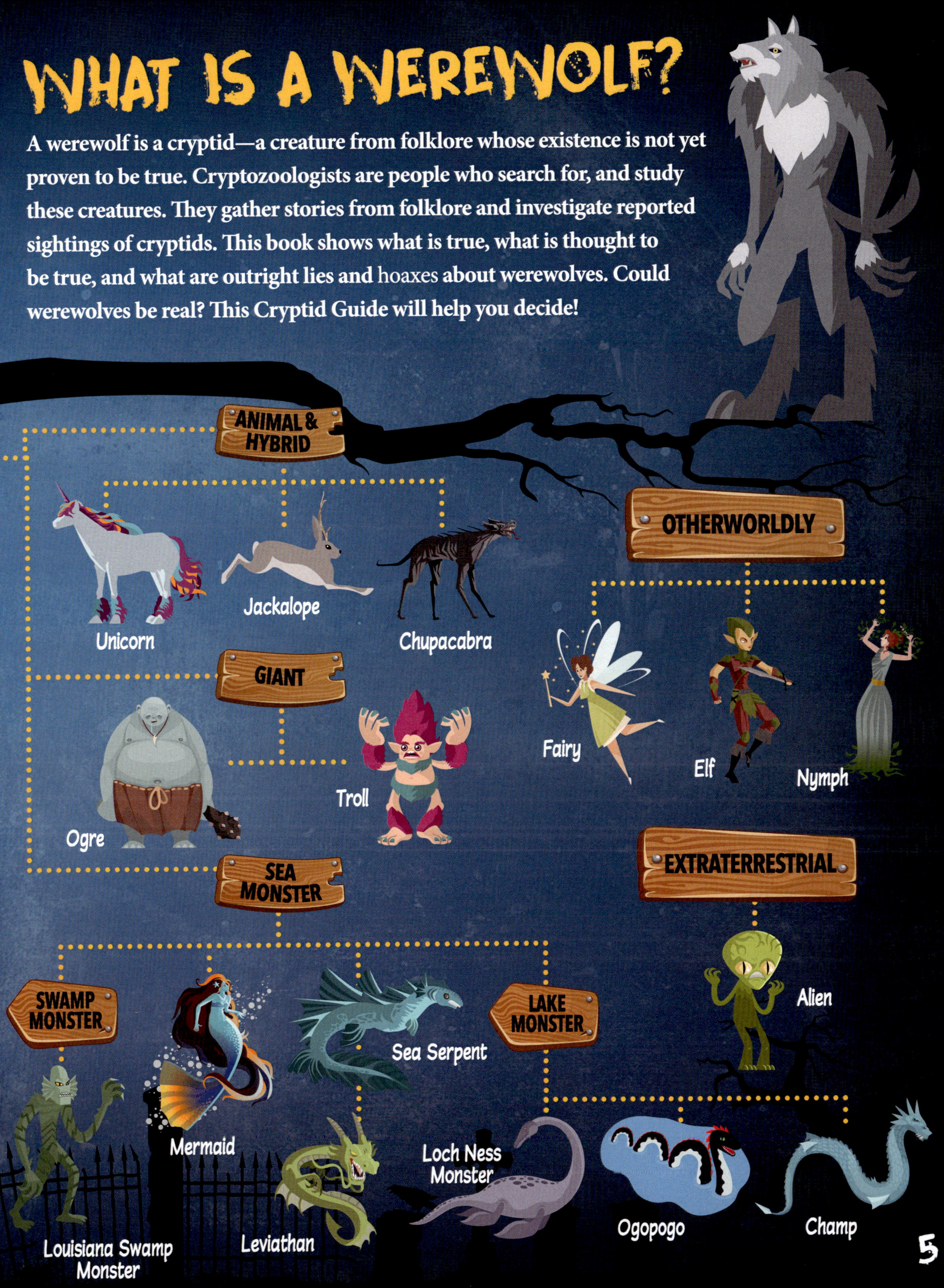

FEAR THE WEREWOLF...

Imagine this: It's long, long ago, before streetlights, electricity, phones, or the Internet. You live on the edge of a forest, on a small farm with sheep, chickens, and other livestock. You walk from the barn one chilly autumn night. The moon is full and you hear the howl of wolves in the distance. A chill runs down your spine. Out of the corner of your eye you see a large, hairy creature with the face of a wolf, but it is walking toward you on two legs—like a human! You run to the house and bolt the door. Your frightened mind tries to make sense of what you just saw. The only thing you can think of to explain the half-wolf, half-human creature are the stories of wolves from ancient myths. Nah, you think, that can't be what you saw. But the next day a nearby farmer says that some of his sheep were killed in the night by a wolf that walked on two legs. Could it be? You tell someone what you saw, and they tell someone else. Soon everyone is talking about the creature and each time the story is retold it gets wilder and wilder...

Stories about werewolves began in places where wolves were top predators. Sadly, real wolves were so feared in Europe that they were hunted to extinction in some places.

WEREWOLF BASICS

According to folklore, werewolves are humans who change into wolves, although in some legends they remain half human, half wolf all the time. People have been telling terrifying stories of werewolves who attack and kill animals and humans since ancient times. And people believed these stories to be true! In fact, between the 1500s and the 1800s, some people in Europe who were accused of murder were found guilty in court of being werewolves! Then, when werewolves started to appear in books and movies and on TV, our ideas about them started to change. Today, werewolves in popular culture are shown as creatures to be pitied, laughed at, or even loved.

WEREWOLF RELATIVES

Beware the werecat!

Werecats are creatures that are half human and half big cat (like a lion, tiger, or leopard). Werecat legends come from places where these big cats are top predators, such as Africa, Asia, and South America.

Werehyenas are no joke!

Werehyenas can be either human-born or hyenas disguising themselves as humans. They can transform at will with the help of a magic stick or a sprinkling of ash. Werehyenas come from African legends.

ANATOMY OF A WEREWOLF

Werewolves—they're hairy, huge, and ferocious. On good days they're human, not much different than you. But on a full moon, watch out! Here's how to spot a werewolf.

According to Swedish folklore, you can tell the difference between a wolf and a werewolf by the way they run. Werewolves run on three legs—their fourth leg is extended behind them like a tail!

Can run upright or on four legs

Curved, sharp fingernails, often reddish

DOG, WOLF, OR WEREWOLF?

When they're in wolf form, werewolves are members of the canine family, which includes wolves and dogs. Although they may look similar, werewolves are much bigger than their canine cousins.

ALASKAN MALAMUTE
Height: 25 inches (64 cm)
Length: 3.5 feet (1 m)

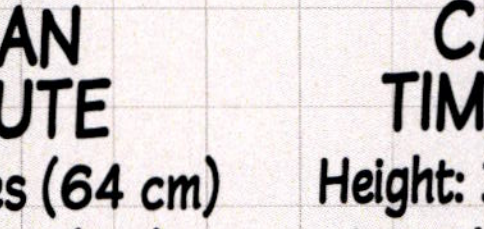

CANADIAN TIMBER WOLF
Height: 30 inches (76 cm)
Length: 5.5 feet (1.7 m)

WEREWOLF
Height: 90 inches (229 cm)
Length: 8 feet (2.4 m)

FACT OR FICTION?

Children have been raised by wolves.

FACT. Not to be confused with werewolves, wolf children are human children who have been raised by wolves. Throughout history, there have been reports of children who were raised by wolves in Germany, India, and Spain. Sometimes, after being rescued by people, these children didn't learn to speak and wanted to return to their wolf packs!

THE WAY OF THE WEREWOLF

Werewolves often get a bad rap—they've been accused of hideous crimes, such as attacking and killing people and animals. They've been hunted down, burned at the stake, and generally shunned by society. Is it any wonder a werewolf would want to keep its wild side hidden?

TELLTALE SIGNS THAT SOMEONE MIGHT SECRETLY BE A WEREWOLF

SOMEONE MIGHT BE A WEREWOLF IF...

- they become troubled or nervous as the full moon approaches
- they are stronger and slightly bigger than an average human
- they look pale and very tired after a full moon
- their houses are trashed and their clothes are ripped after a full moon
- they have yellowish-colored eyes
- their sense of smell, sight, and hearing is better than most people's
- they crave raw meat

SOMEONE MIGHT BECOME A WEREWOLF IF...

- they are bitten by a werewolf
- they are scratched by a werewolf
- they are cursed by a spell
- they drink water from a wolf's paw or pawprint
- they apply a special ointment to their skin
- they wear a cursed wolf belt or cloak

According to some legends, one way to tell if a person is a werewolf is to cut off a piece of their skin to see if there is fur growing underneath!

WEREWOLVES AROUND THE WORLD

In the French-speaking province of Quebec, werewolves are called loup-garou. Werewolf legends likely spread from here to the northern United States.

Werewolves became popular in the United States when they "starred" in Hollywood movies.

Werewolves in Brazil, Argentina, and Paraguay are called luison or el lobizon.

BEWARE: A FACT!

In Armenia, a country in western Asia, a mardagayl is a female werewolf. She is cursed and forced to wear a wolf skin every night for seven years.

WEREWOLVES ON THE MOVE

Werewolf legends first started in Eastern Europe. They spread to other parts of Europe and then to North and South America with settlers who moved to new countries. In 1767 in Quebec City, Canada, the *Gazette* newspaper published a chilling story. A werewolf, or loup-garou as the French settlers called it, had been spotted outside the stone walls of the city at night. Beware, people were told, for the beast was disguised as a beggar to gain entry into the city so it could attack people. Werewolves, they believed, had crossed the ocean aboard ships with French settlers to escape being put on trial for their crimes in France.

TRANSFORMATION

No matter how they transform, it is said that the physical change from human to werewolf is very painful. The word for this transformation is "lycanthropy," which comes from the Greek words *lukos*, meaning "wolf," and *anthropos*, meaning "man."

FIVE MAIN CHANGES THAT HAPPEN DURING TRANSFORMATION

1. Salivary glands grow, muscles ache and grow, body temperature rises, and hair grows extremely fast all over the body.
2. Fingernails grow into long, strong claws as sharp as daggers.
3. Physical size increases—it may even double!
4. Teeth sharpen and grow.
5. Internal organs (such as the heart, liver, and lungs) morph from that of a human to that of a wolf.

PHASES OF THE MOON

The most popular belief today is that werewolves transform every 29.5 days when the moon is full. The moon doesn't have light of its own. Instead, its eerie glow is caused by a reflection of sunlight, which changes depending on where the moon is in relation to the Sun and Earth.

NEW MOON

During a new moon, the moon is between Earth and the Sun. Light reflected from the Sun off the moon can't be seen from Earth.

CRESCENT MOON AND QUARTER MOON

As the moon orbits Earth, different parts of it catch the light from the Sun and reflect it to Earth.

FULL MOON

During a full moon, the moon is on the opposite side of Earth from the Sun. The entire moon is illuminated by light from the Sun.

FACT OR FICTION?

The full moon affects human behavior.

UNKNOWN. The theory that the cycle of the moon influences how humans behave is called the lunar effect. Throughout history, people have believed that the full moon causes humans to act in mysterious ways. Even now, some police officers say that there is more crime during a full moon. The word "lunacy," meaning madness, is rooted in the Latin word *luna* meaning "moon."

SHAPESHIFTERS

Both werewolves and cryptids that are shapeshifters can change from human form to animal form, but there are some important differences between them. Most werewolves cannot stop their transformation from happening. Shapeshifters can take the form of another animal whenever the mood strikes them, and then change back into their human form. Unlike werewolves, when shapeshifters change form, the way they think doesn't change—they are still human.

Here are some examples of shapeshifters from myths, legends, and folklore.

SELKIES

In Scandinavian and Scottish legends, selkies are seals when in water but can shed their seal skins to become human on land. In their human form they are beautiful women who lure fishermen into the sea to marry them.

SKINWALKERS

According to North American Navajo legends, skinwalkers are witches that can change into any animal form. Skinwalkers can be male or female.

SWAN MAIDENS

From Russian folklore, swan maidens are swans that turn into women. In swan maiden legends, a man who wants to marry a swan maiden hides her feathers so she must stay with him.

VAMPIRES

Vampires can turn into bats or wolves. In some Eastern European folklore, vampires, werewolves, and witches are the same creatures. For example, when a Bulgarian werewolf, a vrkolak, is killed, it turns into a vampire.

WITCHES

In folklore around the world, witches can take the form of different animals, including bats, dogs, snakes, and cats. In Scotland, witches can turn into hares and may steal your milk and butter!

FACT OR FICTION?

Werewomen are champions of women's rights.

FACT. In the 1800s in Europe, a type of scary story called Gothic horror began to be written. These stories included female werewolves, or "werewomen." The "wer" in werewolf means "man" in the Old English language, so "werewomen" means the same as "menwomen." Not long after the stories were written, women started to demand the right to vote, the same as men. So some people think that the "menwomen" of the tales stood for women trying to transform into men by demanding equal rights!

HOW TO STOP A WEREWOLF

A werewolf can be difficult to track down because of its double life as a human. But they still need to be stopped before they can strike again. To avoid any unfortunate mistakes, you're going to want to be careful to only kill a werewolf when it is in wolf form.

WEREWOLF HUNTING 101

STEP 1: PACK YOUR KIT

You will need:

- a silver bullet
- a poisonous plant called wolfsbane that acts as a werewolf repellent (in case the werewolf gets the upper hand)
- a breed of dog called an Irish wolfhound

TIP: Irish wolfhounds were bred in Ireland and used to track wolves. They may also offer some protection in case the werewolf attacks you.

STEP 2: FIND A WEREWOLF

You can trying looking...

- at the edges of wooded areas
- near cemeteries
- around military bases

TIP: If the werewolf escapes, you can hide its human clothing to prevent it from turning into a human again.

STEP 3: WAYS TO STOP A WEREWOLF

- Say the werewolf's human name three times to turn it back into a human.
- Give it a saltwater bath to return it to human form.
- The only surefire way to stop a werewolf is with a silver bullet.

TIP: Only a silver bullet will do. This may be because it is a pure metal, whereas other bullets are made from a mix of metals. It may also be because silver is symbolic of the moon in old alchemy texts.

THE LEGENDS BEGIN

As with other cryptids and monsters from legends, it's hard to say exactly when people first started believing in werewolves. One thing we do know is that these myths and legends about werewolves and beings that can shapeshift into wolves go back to ancient times.

Myth vs Legend

Myths are stories from the distant past and are known to be untrue. Myths usually involve gods, creation stories, and moral lessons.

Legends are old tales told as if based on experiences of real people. Legends may have started as truth, but by retelling them over and over again, they become more and more exaggerated.

Don't anger the gods!

MYTH

In the Greek myth of Lycaon, King Lycaon serves the powerful god Zeus human flesh to eat. This angers Zeus, so he kills all of Lycaon's sons with lightning bolts and turns the king into a wolf. Zeus agrees to turn Lycaon back into a human if he can go nine years without hurting anyone.

FACT OR FICTION?

It is illegal to be a werewolf.

FACT. Werewolves were mentioned in laws in some countries in Europe in the Middle Ages. But the word likely referred to people living as outlaws in forests or people who were hired fighters.

MYTH

The first big, bad wolf

Fenrir is a massive wolf from Norse mythology, and the son of the god Loki. According to Norse prophecy, a great battle and natural disasters called Ragnarok will end the world. During Ragnarok, the evil Fenrir will kill the chief god Odin. To prevent this, the Norse gods chained Fenrir up until his special day comes.

The magic wolf cloak

In the Norse Saga of the Volsungs, Sigmund and his son Sinfjotli steal some wolf pelts. When they put them on, they turn into wolves. After attacking and killing many people, Sigmund turns on his son and wounds him. Luckily, Sinfjotli is saved by a raven who delivers a plant leaf with healing powers. When Sigmund and Sinfjotli return to their human form, they burn the pelts so no one can use them to turn into werewolves again.

LEGEND

Warrior wolves

The legend of Laignech Faeland comes from Ireland. Laignech Faeland and his sons were said to be able to turn into wolves who would raid the countryside, killing people and animals. Kings hired them to fight battles for them. According to Irish legends, when Saint Patrick brought the Christian religion to Ireland, Laignech and his sons howled to drown out his voice.

WEREWOLVES ON TRIAL

Europe in the Middle Ages was a bad time to be a werewolf. Werewolves were associated with witchcraft and thought to be doing the Devil's work. People who had been accused of crimes could be tortured into saying that they were werewolves. Here are just a few of Europe's real-life werewolf trials.

Date: 1521

Place: **France**

Name:
Pierre Burgot and Michel Verdun

Accused of:
Swearing loyalty to the Devil, using an ointment to turn themselves into wolves, and killing children

Verdict:
Guilty

Sentence:
Burned at the stake

Date: 1500s

Place: **France**

Name:
Giles Garner, aka "the Werewolf of Dole"

Accused of:
Using an ointment to change into a wolf, killing and eating children

Verdict:
Guilty

Sentence:
Burned at the stake

Date: 1589

Place: **Germany**

Name: **Peter Stubbe**

Accused of:
Turning into a werewolf at night and killing the citizens of Bedburg

Verdict:
Guilty

Sentence:
Tortured, beheaded, and burned

Date: 1603

Place: **France**

Name: **Jean Grenier (a 14-year-old boy)**

Accused of:
Being a werewolf that killed and ate other children

Verdict:
Guilty

Sentence:
Sent to live with monks

Date: 1692

Place: **Present-day Estonia and Latvia**

Name: **Thiess of Kaltenbrun, aka "the Livonian Werewolf"**

Accused of:
Turning into a werewolf and visiting the Devil in Hell, having opinions that went against the teachings of the Church (called heresy)

Verdict:
Guilty

Sentence:
Flogged, or whipped, and kicked out of town

Date: 1800s

Place: **Spain**

Name: **Manuel Blanco Romasanta, aka "the Werewolf of Allariz"**

Accused of:
Being a serial killer. He used the defense of being a werewolf at his trial.

Verdict:
Guilty

Sentence:
Death

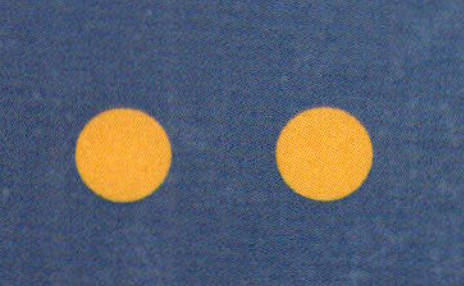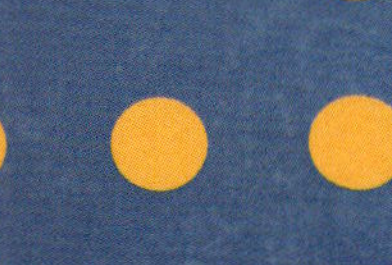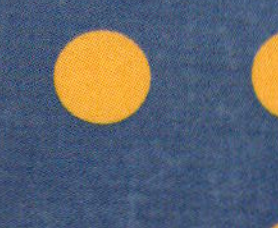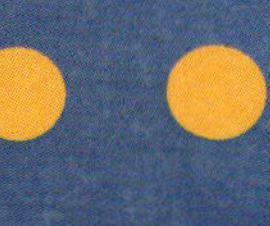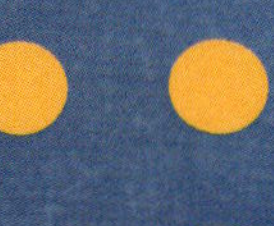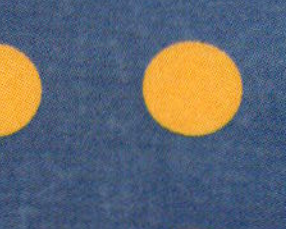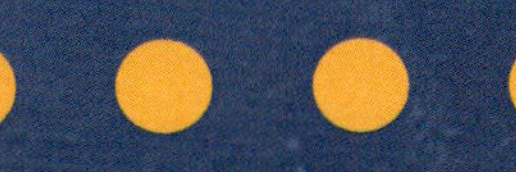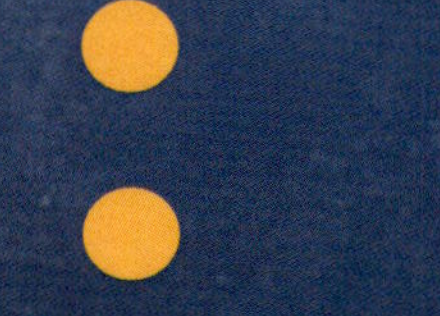

WEREWOLVES MAKE IT BIG

What do you picture when you think of werewolves today? Ferocious beasts to be hunted, or romantic partners, superheroes, and funny guys? The way we think of werewolves has been shaped by books, movies, and comics. This timeline shows how our idea of werewolves has been changed by popular culture over time.

1944

The *House of Frankenstein* movie is released. It stars Frankenstein's monster, vampires, and werewolves. The idea that a werewolf can be killed by a silver bullet comes from this film.

1943

In the film *Frankenstein Meets the Wolf Man,* the idea that the werewolf transforms during the full moon is introduced.

1963

The idea for Wolfman Jack, a popular radio DJ with a gravelly voice, is created. Wolfman Jack would later go on to appear in film and TV.

1973

Marvel character John Jameson, an astronaut from Spider-Man comics, picks up a gemstone on the moon that transforms him into the Man-Wolf when the full moon shines on it.

2007

The Astounding Wolf-Man comic series is launched by Image Comics, featuring a man who becomes a werewolf after being mauled by one. Despite his curse, he tries to use his powers for good.

2006

In *New Moon,* the second book of the teen fantasy romance series *Twilight,* character Jacob Black discovers he is a werewolf. He is protective, caring, and loyal.

START HERE

1800s
Gothic horror stories featuring werewolves are published with themes around the good and evil in people.

1933
The first bestselling adult horror novel featuring werewolves, *The Werewolf of Paris,* is published.

1935
The first mainstream Hollywood horror movie about a werewolf, *Werewolf of London,* is released.

1941
The Wolf Man, a film that made werewolves popular, is released. Our modern-day idea of what a werewolf looks like comes from the special effects in this movie.

1981
Werewolves get funny in *An American Werewolf in London,* a comedy-horror film.

1981
The Howling, a comedy-horror film, is released. There are now eight *Howling* movies in the franchise.

1985
Teen Wolf, a romantic fantasy comedy movie for teenagers, is released. The movie starred one of the most popular teen actors of the '80s, Michael J. Fox.

1999
Werewolf Remus Lupin, aka Moony, appears as a character in *Harry Potter and the Prisoner of Azkaban.* He uses a wolfsbane potion to control his werewolfism.

HUMANOID CRYPTIDS

Humanoid cryptids are any mix of human and animal. These types of cryptids may have some or all of these characteristics:

- the ability to walk on two legs like a human
- human-like facial features, in particular the eyes, as well as a human-sounding voice
- hands, or paws, that are more similar to a human's than an animal's
- near human intelligence

APEMEN

Bigfoot is the best-known of the apemen. Roughly 6 to 9 feet (1.8 to 2.7 m) tall, Bigfoot, or Sasquatch as it is also known, is said to live in forested areas of North America. Bigfoot's cousin, the Yeti, lives in the mountains of Asia and Europe and has white fur.

DOGMEN

Closely related to werewolves, dogmen are any mix of human and canine creature. There have been many reported sightings of dogmen in North America.

GOATMEN

Goatmen are tall creatures that are half human and half goat. Most sightings have been reported in Louisiana, Maryland, and Texas. In ancient Roman mythology, a satyr was a woodland spirit that looked like a man but had a goat's ears, tail, legs, and horns.

DEER PEOPLE

Sightings of deer people have mostly occurred in the United States. They are said to have either the horns and face of a deer with the body of a human, or a human face and the legs and hooves of a deer.

WOLVERINE

Wolverine is a character created by Marvel Comics that first appeared in 1974. Wolverine was created as a Canadian character who is small and fierce like a wolverine. Wolverines are animals related to weasels, badgers, and ferrets. Wolverine is a mutant character whose appearance doesn't change, except for his retractable claws.

THE CRYPTID RECORD

Cryptozoology's #1 Source for Sightings

Werewolves and Dogmen Sighted!

Reported Sightings

Eyewitness accounts are important to people who study cryptids. Cryptozoologists read reports of sightings and interview people who have encountered cryptids. They also read about past sightings to try to put together the full story of a cryptid. Thanks to science, today we know that a human can't transform into a wolf. Instead, cryptozoologists investigate sightings of dogmen, creatures that seem to be half human and half canine. These are just a few real-life sightings of dogmen as they may have been written in newspapers.

Beast of Bray Road | Wisconsin, 2020

Eyewitnesses describe the Beast of Bray Road as a large, wolf-like creature with red eyes. Signs the Beast is nearby include scratch marks on car doors or trunks, and the dead bodies of deer and/or livestock.

Dogman of Fort Custer Michigan, 2000

A sighting of the Michigan Dogman was reported near a military site and a graveyard. The eyewitness said that she was in her car when the creature walked across the road in front of her. She described it as having a body and face similar to a young boy but covered in gray fur, with ears like a German shepherd. The Michigan Dogman is said to be 7 feet (2 m) tall with blue or yellow eyes and a human-sounding howl.

Wolfman of Chestnut Mountain Illinois, 2010

A couple driving on a country road near Galena reported sighting a wolf standing on its hind legs by the side of the road. After making eye contact with the couple, the wolfman dropped to its four legs and ran off at great speed. When the couple looked in their rearview mirror, the creature was behind them, watching their car. The couple quickly drove off.

Mobile Wolf Woman Alabama, 1971

Concerned Mobile citizens called police to report sightings of a strange creature around Davis Avenue and the community of Plateau. There were about 50 reports describing a "wolf woman" that had the face and hair of a woman and the body of a wolf.

Morbach Werewolf Germany, 1988

A United States Air Force unit stationed in Germany called for K-9 backup after discovering the remains of three dead deer and hearing a deep growling coming from the surrounding area. Before backup could arrive, witnesses say that they spotted a large black beast coming toward them before running off into the woods.

Werewolves Explained

Could werewolves be real?

It is possible that some of the animals thought to be werewolves or dogmen are in fact dogs or wolves that have illnesses such as rabies or mange. Rabies is a virus that causes **inflammation** of the brain, resulting in violent behavior. It can be passed from animals to humans through a bite. So a rabid dog or wolf that bit a human could make the human more violent, kind of like a werewolf. A dog with mange could look like it has a more human form in the dark of night. Although rare, dogs have also been known to walk on their hind legs if their front legs are injured.

But what about humans?

There are two known medical conditions that could explain werewolfism. One is hypertrichosis, a rare medical condition in which a person grows hair all over their body, including their face. A real example was a man named Fedor Yevtihiyev who lived from 1864 to 1904. There is also a rare **psychiatric** condition called clinical lycanthropy, in which someone believes that they are an animal.

From Cryptid to Species

For a creature's status to be changed from cryptid to real animal by science, a live specimen has to be found and studied. Sightings, stories, and footprints aren't good enough. Here are some examples of animals that were once cryptids, even though many people knew they were real!

Platypus, cryptid until 1799

Okapi, aka the African unicorn, cryptid until 1901

Komodo dragon, cryptid until 1910

Giant squid, cryptid until 2004

Gorilla, cryptid until 1902

LEARNING MORE

Want to know more about cryptids, myths, and monsters like the ones described in this book? Here are some resources to check out while on your cryptid-hunting quest.

Books

Behind the Legend: Werewolves by Erin Peabody. Little Bee Books, 2017.

Cryptid Creatures: A Field Guide by Kelly Milner Halls. Little Bigfoot, 2019.

Monster Science: Could Monsters Survive (and Thrive!) in the Real World? by Helaine Becker. Kids Can Press, 2016.

TV and Films

Monstrum is a series of videos created by PBS about monsters, myths, and legends.

Find the videos on the PBS website at:

www.pbs.org/show/monstrum/

Websites

The Centre for Fortean Zoology is a cryptozoology organization that researches cryptids from around the world. They produce a weekly TV show, books, and magazines about cryptids.

www.cfz.org.uk/

GLOSSARY

alchemy A medieval type of chemistry that involved making metals and potions

folklore The stories, customs, and beliefs that people of a certain place share and pass down through the generations

hoax An act or object passed off as real and meant to fool someone

illuminate To light up or make something bright

inflammation A response the body has to injury that can cause redness and pain

legend A story that has been passed down through the years. It may have started as true, but became exaggerated over time.

Middle Ages The period of history in Europe that spans the 500s to the 1500s

myths Traditional stories and beliefs, usually about gods and other supernatural figures. Together myths are called mythology.

ointment A soft, oily substance that is usually rubbed on skin as medicine

poisonous A word describing a substance that is harmful to the body

popular culture The movies, music, TV, books, and fashion that everyone is interested in at a certain time

prophecy Something that is predicted to happen in the future

psychiatric Relating to mental or emotional health

repellent A substance used to keep something away, such as bug spray

retractable Able to draw back in

salivary glands Organs in the body that make and control spit

symbolic A word that describes one thing standing for another

INDEX

apemen 4, 26
Beast of Bray Road 28
crimes 10, 13, 15, 20, 22-23
cures 11, 19
curses 11, 12, 29
deer people 27
diseases 30
dogmen 26, 28-29, 30
dogs 9, 17, 19, 26, 29, 30
eyes 8, 26, 28, 29
Fenrir 21
fingernails (claws) 9, 14, 27
fur (hair) 8, 11, 14, 26, 29, 30
goatmen 27
graveyards 19, 29
Laignech Faeland 21
laws 20
loup-garou 12, 13
lunar effect 15
lycanthropy 14, 30
Lycaon 20
mardagayl 12
Michigan Dogman 29
Middle Ages 20, 22
Mobile Wolf Woman 29
moon 6, 9, 11, 14-15, 19, 24
Morbach Werewolf 29
selkie 16
Sigmund and Sinfjotli 21
silver 19, 24
skinwalkers 16
swan maidens 17
teeth 14
vampires 4, 13, 17, 24
volkodiak 13
werecats 4
werehyenas 4
werewomen 12, 17, 29
witchcraft 11, 13, 22
witches 16, 17
wolf belts 11, 13
wolf children 9
wolf cloaks 11, 13, 21
Wolfman of Chestnut Mountain 29
wolfmen 24-25, 29
wolfsbane 19, 25
Wolverine 27
wolves 6, 7, 9, 19, 30